Four Wheels West

A Wyoming Number Book

Written by Eugene Gagliano and Illustrated by Susan Guy

Sleeping Bear Press™

310 North Main Street, Suite 300
Chelsea, MI 48118
www.sleepingbearpress.com

© 2006 Thomson Gale, a part of the Thomson Corporation.

Thomson, Star Logo and Sleeping Bear Press are trademarks
and Gale is a registered trademark used herein under license.

Printed and bound in China.

10 9 8 7 6 5 4 3 2 1

Library of Congress Cataloging-in-Publication Data

Gagliano, Eugene M.
Four wheels west: a Wyoming number book / written by Eugene Gagliano;
illustrated by Susan Guy.
p. cm.
Summary: "Using numbers, much of Wyoming's history, wildlife, and landscapes
are introduced. Topics include two wheel ruts on the Oregon Trail, sugar beets,
sheep, and ancient fossil fish"—Provided by publisher.
ISBN 1-58536-210-7
1. Wyoming—Juvenile literature. 2. Counting—Juvenile literature. I. Guy, Susan,
1948- ill. II. Title.

F761.3.G344 2006
978.7—dc22   2005028280

*Dedicated with love to my grandchildren, Kyla Jade Griffith,
Dakota Wyatt Griffith, and Connor Andrew Gagliano,
and to my friend, Susan Guy, who brought my words
to life with her beautiful illustrations.*

EUGENE

*I would like to thank my husband and my family,
who always believed in me.*

*I would also like to thank Chuck Duncan from the
Wyoming Sugar Company, and the ladies from the Jackson,
Wyoming Chamber of Commerce for their help with this book.*

SUSAN

1 is for the polo field—
America's oldest one.
Come see the polo players.
Enjoy and have some fun.

The nation's first polo field is set at the base of the Big Horn Mountains in Big Horn, southwest of Sheridan, Wyoming. It was originally laid out so that British Army officers could observe horses run the length of the field in order to judge their gaits. The horses were bought for soldiers to use in fighting wars.

A regulation polo field is 300 yards long and 200 yards wide. The goalposts, which are made of light material in case a horse runs into them, are set 24 feet apart at opposite ends of the field.

It takes six months to a year to train a polo pony. Polo ponies must have docility, speed, endurance, and intelligence. The peak age of a polo pony is 9 to 10 years old. The term *pony* is traditional, as it is a full-sized horse.

one

1

For the 250-mile stretch across Wyoming, all the major emigrant trails came together and converged at Fort Laramie.

The Conestoga wagons with their boat-like shape were called the "schooners of the prairie." The wagons ranged from 24 to 26 feet long and stood 10 to 12 feet high, and weighed close to 3,000 pounds.

Conestoga wagons were made of oak or poplar. The tight-fitting bed and sides were caulked with pitch, and could float across a river after the wheels were removed and strapped to the sides.

Mules or teams of horses or oxen pulled the wagons anywhere from 8 to 12 miles a day.

two

2

2 is for the wheel ruts
over hill and dale.
Left by covered wagons
on the Oregon Trail.

Wyoming is one of the four major nesting grounds for the trumpeter swan, the world's largest swan. Yellowstone National Park is one of the best places to see and study them.

Its wings can span eight feet, and a male swan, called a cob, can measure five feet from bill to tail with its neck extended. This swan can sometimes weigh 30 pounds.

The female swan is called a pen and the baby a cygnet.

In 1932 only 69 trumpeter swans were counted in the United States. Today there are almost 10,000 birds.

The trumpeter swan makes the loudest call of any North American bird. Its deep-toned "ko-hoh" call, sounds like a horn.

three
3

3 is for trumpeter swan,
the largest swan of all.
    With graceful snow-white beauty,
it makes the loudest call.

4 is for elk arches
in Jackson Hole's Town Square
made from many antlers,
a sight unique and rare.

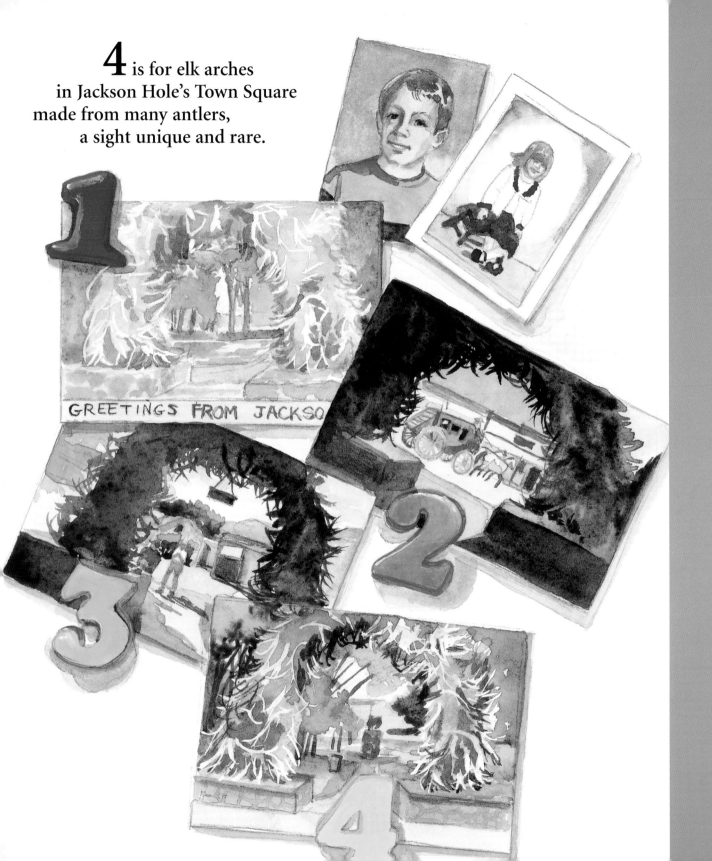

GREETINGS FROM JACKSO

Visitors enter Jackson Hole's Town Square through four unique arches made from hundreds of elk antlers. In winter the snow-covered arches and trees are draped with festive lights. The local Rotary Club planted the park's trees in 1932.

The annual Boy Scout Elk Antler Auction in Jackson Hole is held the third weekend in May. About five tons of antlers are collected annually from the refuge. Elk antlers are used for furniture, belts, and taxidermy; sales attract hundreds of buyers. The antlers sell for an average of $10.00 a pound. Eighty percent of the proceeds help fund the feeding of elk on the refuge.

Afton, Wyoming's best-known attraction, is the world's largest elk antler arch, an 18-foot-high arch that extends over the main street. Built in 1958, it contains 3,011 antlers.

four
4

Wyoming is the 10th largest state in terms of land area, yet it is home to less than 1/600th of the population of the United States. In 2003 the estimated population of the entire state of Wyoming was 501,242 people, which is close in size to the city of Denver, Colorado, with its population of 556,835 people.

Wyoming ranks 50th in population among the states. You guessed it; every other state has more people than Wyoming!

In Wyoming 91% of the land is classified as rural, or countryside. The two main urban, or city, areas are Cheyenne and Casper. The average distance between Wyoming towns is 119 miles.

five

5

5 is for the number
of people per square mile.
Scattered over our state,
we live in western style.

Basque dancers may be accompanied by an accordion, a *pandareta* (tamborine), and a *txistu* (ancient Basque flute pronounced "CHEE-stoo").

The Basque, meaning "the chosen people," come from the Basque area of France and Spain. They became the dominant sheep people in the early days of Johnson County.

Euskera is the language of the Basque people, which many Basques still speak today. They try to preserve their heritage with clubs that pass on the traditions of their dance, costumes, songs, and food at public festivals.

six

6

6 is for Basque dancers
in black and red and white.
Stepping, jumping, twirling—
a very festive sight.

Sheridan, Wyoming serves as head-quarters for all of Holly Hybrids nationwide sugar beet seed research and development. Its objective is to create more productive and disease resistant sugar beet varieties.

While you know sugar is used in baked goods, cereals, soda pop, and other sweet treats, did you also know sugar is used in leather tanning, printers' inks and dyes, and even in textile sizing and finishing? Chemical manufacturers use sugar to grow penicillin.

One ton of sugar beets can make 225 pounds of sugar. Brown sugar is sugar crystals prepared in molasses syrup, giving it the brown color.

The rootlets on a sugar beet can draw nutrients from the soil as deep as six and a half feet.

Did you know that lemons contain more sugar than strawberries?

seven
7

7 is for sugar beets
growing out in fields—
soaking up the sunshine,
producing super yields.

8 is for Black Angus.
They dot the prairie land,
Wyoming's many ranches
are truly vast and grand.

Beef cattle and calves are Wyoming's most valuable agricultural products.

The Angus breed which originated in Scotland are often referred to as *doddies*, a Scotch term for polled or hornless cattle.

George Grant of Victoria, Kansas imported the first four Angus bulls in 1873 to the Kansas prairie. Grant crossed the bulls with native Texas longhorn cows and produced calves that were hornless. These Angus crosses survived well on the winter range and weighed more the next spring.

Black Angus have become an important breed because they are considered hardy and winter well in Wyoming. They mature at an early age and are heavily muscled in the region of the high-priced cuts of beef, and yield a high dressing percentage (the amount of useable meat that is obtained from a live animal).

A heifer is a cow that has never had a calf.

eight
8

Fireweed was named for its ability to grow like a weed in recently burned lowlands or subalpine areas. Its 5-foot, rose-pink spires bloom during the summer. They grow from rhizomes (underground root-like stems), which take hold deep in the soil, below the duff. The duff is the layer of soil which heats to lethal temperatures during a fire.

In 1988 Yellowstone National Park experienced the worst fire season in the park's history due to the heat of summer, extreme drought, and high-speed warm winds. A total of 1.2 million acres burned.

At first park rangers allowed the fires to burn because it's part of forest ecology. Ecology is the relationship between living things and their surroundings. Forest fires clear away old trees to make way for new plants and trees. For example, heat from the fire causes lodgepole pine seeds to pop from their cones.

Fireweed helped to reclaim the land after the fire.

nine

9

9 is for fireweed,
lovely purple spires
that sprouted in the park
after Yellowstone's fires.

10 is for sage grouse
which dance and strut about.
See their courtship ritual
in springtime if you're out.

Wyoming's most plentiful and widely distributed native game bird is the sage grouse, North America's largest grouse. Wyoming is considered the "sage grouse capital" of the United States.

Males have large mustard-colored throat pouches that are inflated with air during their traditional courting ritual. The female grouse shows submissive behavior like slimmed plumage and silent movements during the ritual to avoid male hostility characteristic of male-male encounters.

The sage grouse, like the mule deer and antelope, depend on sagebrush lands for survival, and Wyoming has more sage than any place else in North America. You won't find sage grouse where sage doesn't grow. In winter sage grouse, also called sage hens, depend entirely on the soft evergreen leaves and shoots of the sagebrush to survive.

Sagebrush produces a volatile oil that acts as a natural herbicide preventing competition from other plants. This sweetly pungent bush grows from the deserts to 10,000-foot mountains.

ten
10

The mineral extraction industry is the main driver of Wyoming's economy with the production of coal, methane gas, natural gas, and oil. In 2002 Wyoming ranked 7th among all the United States in the production of crude oil, with 54.7 million barrels.

On Wyoming's state seal, the words "Livestock," "Mines," "Grain," and "Oil" represent Wyoming's wealth.

The first recorded discovery of oil in Wyoming was an oil spring near Hilliard, when Fort Bridger was established in 1842. However, Wyoming's first oil well was drilled in 1884 southeast of present-day Lander. Petroleum, or crude oil, is found near sedimentary rock. The word petroleum comes from two Latin words meaning "rock" and "oil."

Wyoming's first oil refinery was built in Casper in 1895. An oil refinery prepares oil after it comes from the well and turns it into petroleum products like gasoline and kerosene.

eleven
11

11 is for oil rigs
bobbing up and down,
pumping on the rangeland
or just outside of town.

12 is for the only trees
once found in old Cheyenne.
Many of the trees today
were planted there by man.

In 1876 Mrs. Nannie Steel reported only 12 trees growing in Cheyenne, the state capital.

In 2004 a tree inventory/evaluation was done in the central part of Cheyenne. It showed that the Populus species (cottonwood, poplar, and aspen) comprised 19.8% of the inventoried trees, the largest percentage of species. The cottonwood, the state tree, has waxy leaves that help it to retain moisture during the hot summer months.

Wyoming's state capitol, located in the heart of Cheyenne, resembles the National Capitol in Washington, D.C., but it has a gold dome that shines in the sun. The cornerstone of the building was laid on May 18, 1887.

A mounted bison, the third largest bison to ever be listed in the Boone and Crocket Book of Records, can be seen in the state capitol building in Cheyenne.

twelve
12

See the flock of **20** lambs
as they jump and play,
bouncing happy bundles
on a springtime day.

Sheep provide meat in the form of lamb and mutton, wool for clothing and carpets, and milk for drinking and cheese making.

In 2003 Wyoming was the third leading state in sheep production with 460,000 animals, and second in wool production.

Sheep are even-toed hoofed animals that chew their cud and can live up to 20 years.

The first sheep came to Wyoming in 1870. Some ranchers wanted sheep, so like cattle drives, sheep herds were driven to Wyoming from the West Coast.

twenty

20

Many hot air balloons can be seen at the Annual Riverton Rendezvous Rally in July. The city of Riverton is surrounded by the Wind River Indian Reservation. People ballooning at the rally get a great view of the Wind River Mountains, the state's longest and highest mountain range. The name *Wind River Mountains* originated as a Crow Indian reference to the warm Chinook winds that blow down the Wind River Valley.

The Wind River Mountain range runs along the Continental Divide. On the east side of the mountains the Wind River flows toward the Atlantic Ocean, while on the west side of the mountains the Green River flows toward the Pacific Ocean.

Hot air balloons are used for commercial flights, pleasure rides, business advertisements, and sports. Sometimes people get married on hot air balloons.

thirty

30

In the sky are 30 hot air balloons in flight— rainbow colors airborne make a lovely sight.

40 elk are grazing
along a mountain side.
A mighty antlered bull elk
protects his herd with pride.

The world's largest single elk herd is found in Wyoming.

Near the border of Grand Teton National Park, the 25,000-acre National Elk Refuge provides a winter home to 7,500 elk every year. They remain there for about six months. The elk are fed supplementally if forage is not available.

In winter, horse-drawn sleigh rides are available to take visitors for a close-up look at the elk herd.

The Shawnee Indian word for elk is "wapiti," which means "white rump." The Algonquin Indians also referred to elk as wapiti.

The Shoshone Indians hunted the elk for meat and clothing. The elk horns were used to sharpen knives and arrow points, and elk teeth were used to decorate their clothing.

In autumn, during the mating season, or rut, the bugling sounds of the bull elk echo throughout the mountains.

forty
40

Look, **50** giant windmills.
Rowed soldiers near the sky
are generating energy
as the wind blows by.

The High Plains of Wyoming has an endless supply of wind, where you will find wind farms—collections of windmills used to produce electricity. Hundreds of windmills are needed to produce significant amounts of electricity.

The Foote Creek Rim I project in southeast Wyoming was dedicated on Earth Day, April 22, 1999. The turbines at the project, where the average wind speed is 25 miles per hour, can produce enough electricity to power 2,700 homes.

The turbines can produce electricity with wind speeds from 8-65 miles per hour. If winds are above 65 miles per hour the turbines automatically shut down to prevent damage. Electronic control systems point each turbine into the wind and adjust the pitch of the blades to make the best use of the wind at any speed.

fifty
50

The state fossil, the Knightia, was adopted on February 18, 1987 due largely to the efforts of elementary student Fred Hurlburt of Cheyenne. He spoke in front of the State House of Representatives and State Senate to promote House Bill 361 for the adoption, as well as promoting it on local radio shows.

Fifty million years ago a large body of fresh water covered parts of Wyoming and Utah. Knightia swam in these waters. They died in masses and sank to the bottom and were covered with sediment and became fossilized.

Rich deposits of fish fossils were exposed during the building of the Union Pacific Railroad. Part of that area near Kemmerer has been protected and has become Fossil Butte National Monument.

sixty
60

60 ancient fossil fish—
these Knightia discovered
were buried in the sandstone
until they were uncovered.

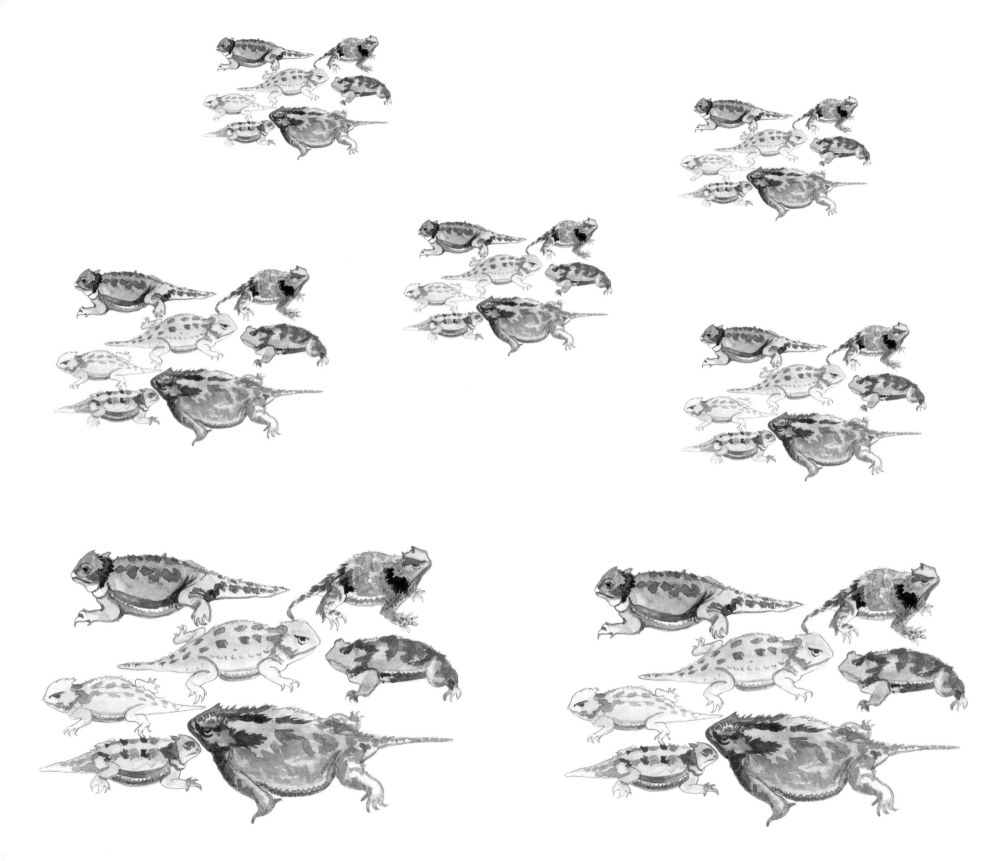

70 horned lizards
        are basking in the sun,
    waiting for a passing ant
                to lick up with their tongue.

Wyoming's rough terrain is home to the Northern Short-Horned Lizard. This diurnal creature, or one that is active during the day time, is dull-colored, brown or gray, with horns that are little more than short, stubby nubbins. A single row of fringe scales can be found along each side of its abdomen.

The horned lizard, often called the horny toad, eats sow bugs, spiders, and other insects, especially ants. High temperatures are needed to stimulate its appetite.

If threatened, the horned lizard can squirt blood from the forward corner of its eyes for a distance of several feet.

seventy
70

The world's largest piece of jade, a 3,336-pound nephrite jade boulder, was found near Lander in the 1940s. Jade was adopted as the state gemstone on January 25, 1967.

Jade is a semiprecious stone that comes in various shades of green "apple," "emerald," "leek," or "bluish-green." Pure jade is white. Any other color of jade has impurities in it.

It is one of nature's toughest minerals, even harder than steel.

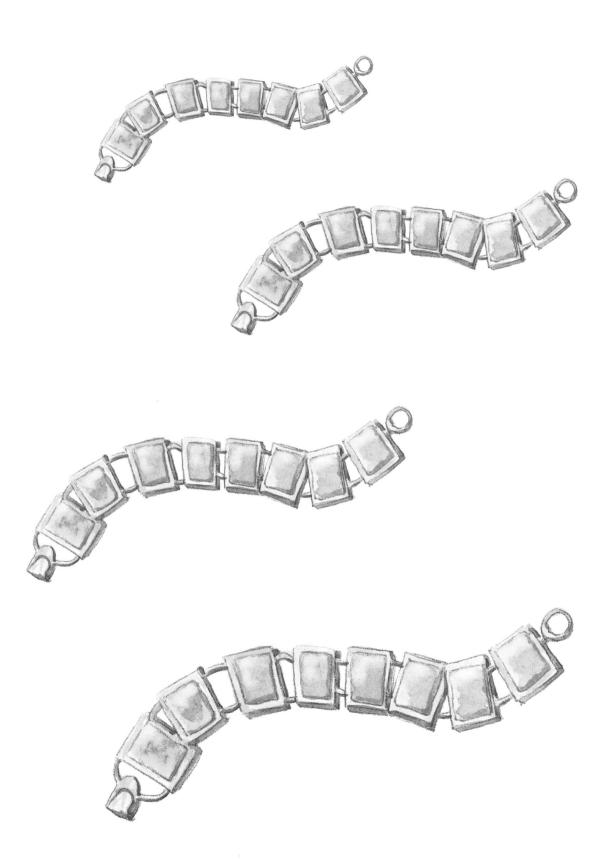

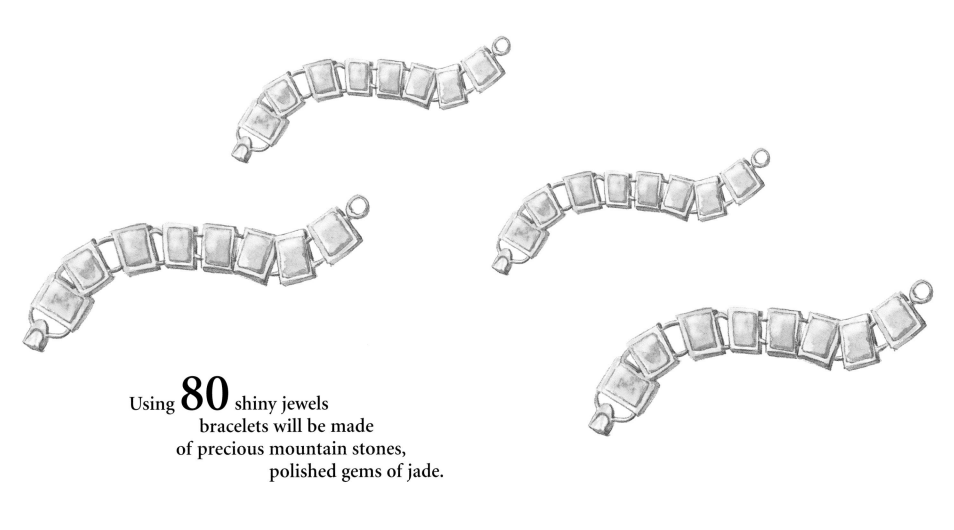

Using **80** shiny jewels
bracelets will be made
of precious mountain stones,
polished gems of jade.

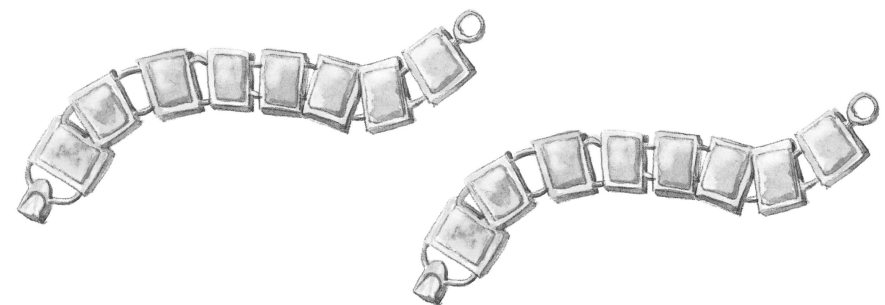

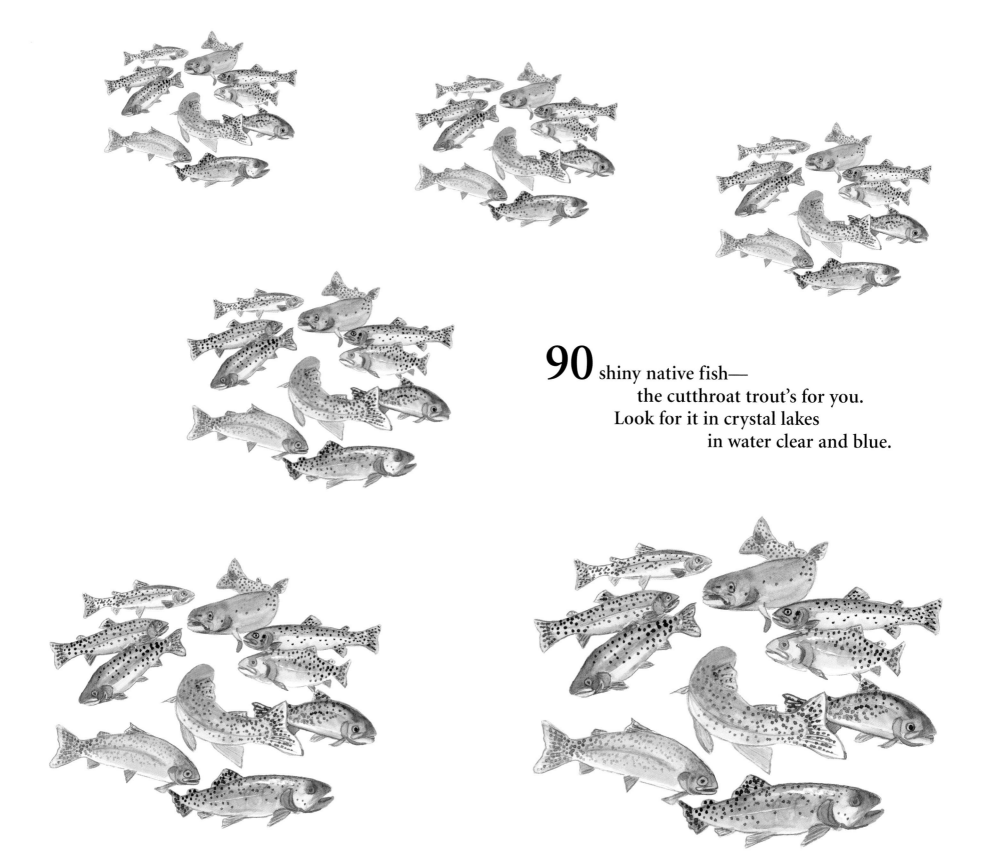

90 shiny native fish—
    the cutthroat trout's for you.
Look for it in crystal lakes
    in water clear and blue.

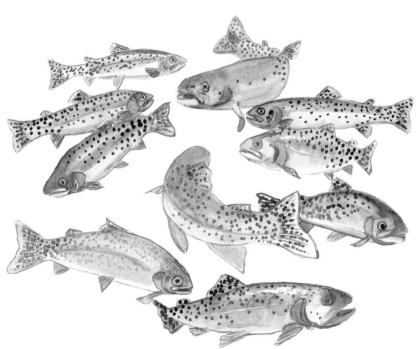

The cutthroat trout is a native of the Rocky Mountains and became Wyoming's state fish on February 18, 1987. It is an aggressive feeder and popular with fly-fishers because it is a scrappy fighter. It grows 10 to 20 inches in length and has a crimson slash on either side of the throat, below the lower jaw.

There are four subspecies: the Snake River trout, the Yellowstone trout, the Colorado River trout, and the Bonneville trout, which is the rarest.

ninety
90

Wyoming's state mammal, the bison, was adopted on February 23, 1985.

In 1894 the government made a law to protect the remaining bison in Yellowstone National Park, which is still home to one of the few large wild populations of bison.

The Durham Buffalo Ranch near Wright has one of the largest private herds in the country, with 3,500 head.

Bison, nearsighted animals with a keen sense of smell and hearing, are the largest mammals in North America, weighing up to 2,000 pounds.

Commonly called buffalo, these shaggy beasts are technically bison. The only true buffalo are the water buffalo of Southeast Asia.

Pioneers burned bison droppings, or chips, for fuel. The dried chips burned fiercely with a minimum of smoke.

one hundred
100

100 bison in a herd
in Yellowstone, their home.
Protected by the government,
these shaggy beasts do roam.

Eugene Gagliano

Gene Gagliano, the "teacher, who dances on his desk," was the recipient of the International Reading Association's 2004 Wyoming State Literacy Award. Gene's other books include *C is for Cowboy, A Wyoming Alphabet, Secret of the Black Widow, Inside the Clown,* and *Falling Stars.* He is a member of the Society of Children's Book Writers and Illustrators and the Wyoming Writers. Gene and his wife, Carol, live at the base of the Big Horn Mountains in Buffalo, Wyoming. He and Carol have enjoyed singing with the Polyester Blends, a professional musical group for 15 years. Gene enjoys making his educational and entertaining school visits, as well as hiking, gardening, canoeing, and painting.

Susan Guy

Award-winning artist Susan Guy is known for her colorful paintings of equine and western themes. Her work has been displayed in numerous galleries and exhibitions across the country including the Arts for the Parks competition in Jackson, Wyoming and the American Academy of Equine Art in Lexington, Kentucky. She has work included in the permanent collections of the Phippen Museum in Arizona, and the Pierce Western Art Collection at Navarro College in Texas. She is a Signature Member of the American Academy of Women Artists, and the Society of Animal Artists. She and her husband, Wesley, share their Buffalo, Wyoming home with their two dogs.